Best wishes,

Ann
(Barefoot)

STANDING ON YOUR HEAD

Rosemary Schonfeld

MINERVA PRESS
ATLANTA LONDON SYDNEY

STANDING ON YOUR HEAD

ISBN 1 86106 522 1

First Published 1998 by
MINERVA PRESS
Sixth Floor
Canberra House
315–317 Regent Street
London W1R 7YB

Printed in Great Britain by Minerva Press

STANDING ON YOUR HEAD

In memory of my grandparents Růžina Schönfeldová (née Weber) and Paul Schönfeld, and my uncles, Drs Mořic and Egon Schönfeld, who died in Auschwitz and other concentration camps.

Acknowledgements

I want to thank the editors at Minerva Press for their encouragement, and Marianne Hester for her love, patience and support.

Contents

Helium Balloon	9
The Ballad Of Annie Acorn And Ethelburp Gunglegook	12
I Wish	19
My Application	22
For Sandy	23
The Fool, The Toller, The Rubber Stamp, The Town	27
For Jana	32
You Are But Young	37
The Parcel	39
Perhaps	41
For Sharon	45
My Muse	47
The Dreamer	50
Wear R U	54
The Clown On The Merry-Go-Round	56
The Granite Bird	60

Helium Balloon

In the thickest nebulous
In the driest wet
By the boring fabulous
Near the credit debt

There you'll find the seaside wine
And drown in sandy air
When the helium balloon
Is too much weight to bear

You've travelled further standing still
Than the planes high in the sky,
But you wait for the thunder
And all you hear's a sigh,

But if you wait for yesterday
Or cry for what's not said,
You'll be there when nothing comes
Standing on your head

All you want is everything
All you fear is pain
Holding on until the dawn
These things never change.

Then one more time you're reminded
One more time you think you might find it
Can't wait run out the door
Saying 'See you later, I want more.'

Then you're in the thickest nebulous again
In the driest wet again
Bored by the fabulous again
Saying 'When will I ever learn, oh when?'

Again you find the seaside wine
And drown in sandy air
Ride in the helium balloon
And sink into somewhere.

You've travelled further standing still
And you didn't even try,
But you turn again
You're standing high and dry,

But if you wait for yesterday
Or cry for what's not said
You'll be there when nothing comes
Standing on your head.

The Ballad Of Annie Acorn And Ethelburp Gunglegook

from the collected letters of Annie Acorn, Volume XI

This story is a sad one, or a good one, it depends
If you see it down a line or from around the bend
The end is the beginning, or maybe it's the middle
And only fools will think this verse was written as a riddle.

There lived in the suburbs of an English-speaking land
A woman who could sing and play guitar with the wrong hand
No one understood her many talents there at home
So she set out to be famous and successful all alone.

Before she found a manager, her name was short and boring
The name she chose and kept till fame stopped anybody snoring
'Ethelburp Gunglegook' when spoke or shown in lights
Made people stop and notice any hour of the night.

Ten years later found her at the high point of the tree
Singing country music and as rich as rich can be
In interviews and articles her story was oft told
But certain information she decided to withhold.

For instance, why were there three years
She would not speak about
Except to say she'd just left home and was a gadabout?
And why is she still living in her manager's abode?
Her manager's a woman, well, it breaks the social code.

To this last query Ethelburp replies most icily
'I choose this situation as it suits me very nicely!'
And no reporter dared to venture past this boundary
Lest the sharp tongue of this star made of him a mockery.

The manager could never be from Ethelburp's side torn
The name of this companion, confidante, was Annie Acorn
She would be there at her side for galas and great fêtes
Where always Ethel's virtues Annie would elucidate

And if you took the time to read her every album cover
You'd find the dedication on each one to none other
Than 'the manager who clearly made me what I am today –
The one who keeps inspiring me with insights wise but
gay.'

For many years the two of them could ride a wave of glory
For a normal singer at this point would end the story
But a dark cloud full of malice one day entered their blue
sky
Into their golden ointment flew a fat and sickly fly.

It began in the week of the Grammy celebrations
Ethelburp and Annie were amidst the preparations
For the speech of acceptance, for Ethelburp would win
'Best Female Country Vocalist' most surely, again.

First Ethelburp bemoaned a sore throat and aching head
And when she ran a fever Annie put her straight to bed
Despite her protestations Ethel's temperature had soared
'You are too ill and simply must not move,' Annie
    implored.

Now Annie had a business mind as clever as they come
She could saunter in with nothing and leave with royal
    sums
Right away she phoned the press to tell her client's plight
'Publicity like this will sure boost sales overnight.'

The press arrived believing Ethelburp might shortly die
And hovered there like vultures for a corpse to be wheeled
    by
Annie kept them posted on the mercury's decline
Dramatically announcing, finally, 'She will be fine.'

Dejectedly the press withdrew without a decent story
No funeral or tears or deaths by means distinctly gory
But one reporter on a hunch did not leave with the others
Invisibly he slipped into some bushes for a cover

And underneath the window ledge of Ethelburp's sickroom
He overheard a conversation later re-illumed.
Here the fat and sickly fly rubbed his hands together
And settled with his notebook for a story told forever.

'Oh honey pie,' there came the breathy, sultry voice of
Annie,
'You should have seen the press eat up
My comments just like candy
The world is waiting for you to appear tomorrow morn
Splashed across the headlines and obituary columns.'

'Annie darling, my true love, you monetary wizard
Only you successfully a risk like this would hazard.
Where would I be without you? Ah, but really I do know
I'd still be poor and lonely as I was those years ago.

'I remember when we met,' said Ethelburp, oblivious
To the pair of ears absorbing this with motives so
malicious,
'I'd lost all hope that I would be a famous country star
I'd learned I was a lesbian and hung around the bars.

'What else was I to do? There was no room in country
charts
For me to sing the pleasures of a woman in my heart.
In order to be famous every woman must agree
To sing about how endless men have brought them to their
knees

'Or how a woman's life shines in a glory quite religious.
If ecstasy is kissing one face rough and hard and strigose
How could I sing about these things when men just make
me ill?
For three full years I had no dream I thought I could fulfil

'And then you came into my life, you took me home one
night
And heard me singing in the bath, I felt so warm and bright
You listened to my tale of woe and said assuredly
"You could be rich if you let *you* replace that vile *he*.

'"You need not give away the fact you never touch a man
All the lyrics can be changed, ambiguously planned
Just let me handle your affairs and never will you starve
I'll see to it you leave this life of rotting in the bars."'

The reporter in the bushes was the first one thus to know
Why there are three full years that Ethelburp
Will ne'er disclose.
He figured now he had enough material to write
An exposé so sellable he would be set for life.

The morning papers came around, not mentioning her ills
Instead the headlines were so large
That one whole page was filled
'TOP COUNTRY SINGER IS A PERVERT' every paper
read
And all the copies Annie brought to Ethelburp in bed.

THE SPHERE
Ethelburp
FANTASTIC
SAY 4,000
DAILY SQUARE
Ethelburp
AMAZING
PURPLE PRESS
Ethelburp
RAG
Ethelburp

THE SPHERE
TOP COUNTRY
SINGER IS
A PERVERT
DAILY SQUARE
TOP COUNTRY
SINGER IS
A PERVERT
PURPLE PRESS
TOP COUNTRY
SINGER IS
PERVERT

'Damn it all!' said Ethelburp, still a little pale,
'Tell me Annie, will this news be helpful to my sales?'
'I doubt it very much, my dear, I think the opposite
The stores will burn your records, love,
In short I fear that's it.'

'Oh well,' shrugged Ethelburp as she drank her morning
    tea
As long as we're together that's what matters most to me.
At last we can stop playing at this ludicrous charade
A strain it was and all the time I felt like such a fraud.

'Annie we are rich enough, it surely does not matter
Anything your heart desires I'll serve you on a platter
Why, we could even start our own recording company
We've got this far, there is no end to possibilities.'

This is where the story stops, though temporarily
Pausing here was chosen rather arbitrarily
For Ethelburp and Annie withdrew from society
And their stories carry on, more rebellious and more free.

I Wish

I wish I were a lonely owl
In the silent night
Knowing when I chose to speak
I gave a chilling fright

I wish I were a jellyfish
Floating in the sea
Watching swimmers rush away
As soon as they saw me

I wish I were a thorny tree
Living near a ranch
Laughing when the cowboys pricked
Their pride against my branch

And if I were a bumble-bee
Sitting on a flower
Those a thousand times my size
Would shudder at my power

GLUE

I wish I were a dream which ended
With the dawning light
Then I'd stand as Reason throwing
Facts against the night

I wish I were a wardrobe or
A bucket full of glue
I wish I could be anything
Except in love with you.

My Application

I sent my application to the Great One in the sky
And asked for some assistance in my task of getting by
I'd noted my credentials in the column marked 'U Fool'
And listed very carefully my papers from Dream School.

It's been rather a long time since it went by cosmic post
In fact sometimes I do despair it's well and truly lost
For surely no Great Keeper of the secrets there above
Could possibly consider my fine points not good enough?

For Sandy

I am not unaware, no I'm not unaware
How you tread the unknown path
For rivers flowing both ways at once
Wrapping yourself in a laugh

The night sounds may roar and you wake long before
The sun lifts itself into the sky
You'll breakfast on soup of invisible roots
And a wishing well sky in a pie

You dream and you guess, 'Would I know any less
If I'd known what I don't know before?
Would I glow and flow in a rainbow of light
With a map of my life on the floor?

'The forest has changed, something's quite rearranged
The landmarks I knew so well
When I look in the pond, my reflection is gone
There's a sign saying "Never Will Tell".'

So you stumble and leap, and dash and creep
And feed on a moonbeam quiche
The question is 'Yes?', the answer's a test,
A silence, a whisper, a screech

In your secret lair you hide away
While the antics of others go mad
And you're watching the elephant dance on a flower
With a wand, a tuxedo, and hat

And rabbits cruise by in their pink limousines
Wearing shades to protect their eyes
And the owl is computing a mistress scheme
For robbing the world of its lies

The fox is colluding the night before
With the hounds for next day's hunt
Speaking of pacifist tactics in war
And how that is what they all want

There's a kangaroo lost its way down south
It took one leap too long
It soared over oceans and with open mouth
Landed sideways singing a song

And the frog sits by her evening fire
Eating toast and smoking dope
Saying 'Toast is toast is a piece of toast,
But can I really cope?'

And the brass band plays for days and days
Variations on one theme
In perfect pitch with the forest witch
Dressed in robes of emerald green

She glides about, within, without
Conducting the Madness Fugue
With a chorus of stars, a harmony from Mars
And her cosmic witch's Moog

She reaches the heights of all planets' delights
Then cues for the whispering wind
While all creatures sway to the rhythms she plays
Over, and over, again

All those in this lair have found their way there
By walking a magical mile
Direction unknown, where the walking stick's flown
And bicycles sleep for a while

And there you will sit, questioning it
But the question and answer's the same
And you're outside of and part of it
On your own spinning wheel of change

I am not unaware, no I'm not unaware
How you tread the unknown path
For rivers flowing both ways at once
Wrapping yourself in a laugh

The Fool, The Toller, The Rubber Stamp, The Town

There was a Fool who lived in a castle made of dreams
He wired the house so nothing was exactly as it seems
He rigged the drawbridge, drained the moat
And filled it with his cares
Anyone there passing had to pay a ransom fare

The Toller was a taxman seeking pounds for stale ideas
His Rubber Stamp said 'Endless' for it spoke of endless
  fears
The Rubber Stamp complained of how it never went to
  Town
The Toller said the Town was grieved and wrote its story
  down

The story of the Town is sad and bound to make you weep
It made so many people cry it's locked away for keeps
The Toller knew it off by heart and told his Rubber Stamp
They settled down with a keg of beer and a cosy, rosy lamp.

The Town's Story

'I was sitting here enjoying the attentions and the life
Of a people born to luxury and tolerance of strife
But no one seems to realise I'm tired and I'm worn
All the glamour that I offer is jaded and forlorn

‘I live upon a river from whom nobody can drink
And I live within an atmosphere where nobody can think
The politicians talk all day of hooligans and thugs
Then wander home and hit their wives and still feel very smug.’

The Toller had now placed a pail to catch his baleful tears
He’d made his Rubber Stamp so damp its message was not clear
The Rubber Stamp now called to mind the story that its mother
Had told it when she simply could not think of any other

‘Hopeless is and Hopeless was a bandit in the night
Robbing dreams and pushing stars completely out of sight.

‘Hopeless came and Hopeless stayed, delivering his speech
People yawned and people cried, but no one would beseech

‘No one yet has caught him, though he will not move an inch
No one can implore him, and nought can make him flinch

‘Everyone sat mutely while he spoke the words again
His words in air like paper ’neath a sickly, oozing pen

'He took and took, they sat and sat, and no one dared to
speak
He took some hands, he took some eyes, he even took next
week

'He took their voices, leaving them too quiet for a prayer
He took half of their knowledge, but left them their despair

'He filled his empty sack with all this booty for his ride
His sack with priceless treasure, locked away inside

'Yes, Hopeless is and Hopeless was a bandit in the night
Robbing dreams and pushing stars completely out of sight.'

In these respective mournful states, the Toller and the
Stamp
Finished up the keg of beer beside the rosy lamp
The Fool within the castle smiled loudly to himself
And put the Chateauneuf du Faff up on the shelf

He leaves the Toller and the Stamp to work within their
bureau
Though fool he seems he never leaves
His Problems for the morrow
As soon as one besets him be it Folly, State, or Person
He sends them to the Toller with an oath to reimburse
them

And there the Toller groans and moans with his tears so damp
And promises to ease the Problems with his Rubber Stamp
All Problems started out with hopes of brilliant careers
Some dream of spreading chaos in this vale of endless tears

Others might become a War, a Faction, or a Plague
While lesser Problems drift about, opting to be vague
The Fool he does not care, he has his Toller and his Stamp
And no one can get near him 'less he lowers down his ramp

And there he lives, he's lived there
Almost since the year was One
While all else crumbles round him,
He lives on, and on, and on.

For Jana

I was sitting at home alone one night
Rocking back and forth in my chair.
It was a cold, grim, sleet filled, moonless night
With a heaviness in the air.

So naturally it made me jump
When I heard a knock on my door.
Who could be out on this dismal night?
What earthly reason for?

I went to the window and pulled back the drape
Just a little, to see who was there.
The fog was heavy and vaguely I saw
A figure's outline appear.

I could make out the form of a woman alone
Silently facing my door.
Relieved, I rushed to let her in
I was halfway across the floor,

When I heard the notes of a clarinet
Wafting into my ears
Sweet dulcet sounds like an African flute
At dusk, when the sun disappears.

My mind went wandering to distant lands
That live in my head, yes those
Spectacular silhouettes of mountains sharp
Yet gentle in their repose.

The pitch went higher and as it rose
I swear someone started to cry
Then it went down low, step by step
Diminishing into a sigh

The tears came slowly to my eyes
As I began to weep
The tune aroused a veiled sorrow
Lying neglected, asleep

My spirit lay heavy from this last refrain
My heart desired only relief
Craving for solace I was, when the tone
Contorted itself to a screech.

I'd never heard such a sequence of notes
As mad as the Mad Hatter's Tea
D sharp, G flat, two octaves below
An ear piercing, harmonic, high C.

I tried to follow this elusive trail
Of a shattering, maddening mind,
When subtly and tastefully again it changed
And left the adventure behind

For low tones of lush and lingering song
That filled me with longing and fire
I sensed a lover calling me for
Her insatiable, passionate desire.

The music slid up to what key I don't know
But ever so lightly it moved,
Making me laugh at the humour of life
And how nothing of worth is approved.

The satire in which we all live became clear
In one or two phrases, that's all
And then came a darkness pervading the sound
That spoke of the fear in us all.

From this eerie mood the music rose
To a pitch of anger untold
The fury of all deeds unjust and cruel
Of murders for vengeance and gold.

I could bear no more multifarious sounds
And messages deep and wise
I had to know who was making these tunes
I must see her with my own eyes.

I ran to the door and flung it wide
To see her features clear
I saw where there had stood her form
But she had disappeared.

I must have paused for minutes, stunned
And still, in disbelief
The rain had stopped, the moon shone full
The stars glowed with relief,

But nowhere in my range of sight
Was any human form
I know she'd been, but now she was
Most irretrievably gone

I sometimes wonder, a long time hence
Who the woman might have been
Was she a friend I've yet to meet?
A time transported being?

But I guess she never wanted me to know who she was
Because
Because
Because

You Are But Young

You are but young, yes that I know
Though with the words hurled to and fro
You'd have me think you know it all
That winter comes before the fall

But if I knew all I said
I'd not be with you here in bed
And you'd not have a second chance
To lead me this appalling dance.

things,
all sorts
with me,
you had
many

The Parcel

I'm going to make a parcel up
And leave it at your door
I'll fill it with all sorts of things
You'll never want for more

When you first unwrap you'll find
Your promises for me
Covered with your words of love
And ideology,

Next you'll find a bundle of
Deception, tricks and lies
Wrapped in pinky paper
And looking like a prize,

Then there'll be a package of
The years you had with me
But this one is all torn now
A pile of debris,

Oh, and there's a box sealed tight
Containing but a few
Of the many endless tears
I've shed over you.

There's more besides, but I don't wish
To ruin the surprise
Maybe it will help you once
To open up your eyes

I'll leave this great big parcel, dear,
All glistening and neat
There upon your doorstep
That leads down to the street,

And when you open up your door
And take an outward step
I hope you find my parcel, dear,
And trip, and break your neck!

Perhaps

A whisper of tropical sunset and dreams
An island of dawn song and treasure unseen
Laughter and mystery
Electric delights
Whispering, beckoning us in the night

The first few bars of a magical song
Luring, alluring, drifting along
Promises silent
Wafts of a tune
Melody shifting, as sand on a dune

Whirling tornadoes of loving desire
Sweeping enchantment soft touches inspire,
Fingertips lightly
Enthralling but tame
Guiding the eye to the path whence it came.

A shadow was dancing, dancing aloud
Circling and calling us into the crowd
Drawing us closer
Nearer to flames
Teasing and daring again and again.

A dreamer awakens, surprised by the light
That crept through the shades on the window of night
Blinking the sleep
Away from her eyes
The light is a memory of lifetimes gone by.

Perhaps in the future, perhaps in the past
Perhaps it's the present which always comes last
Prisms of diamond
Reflecting a time
When I would be yours, and you would be mine.

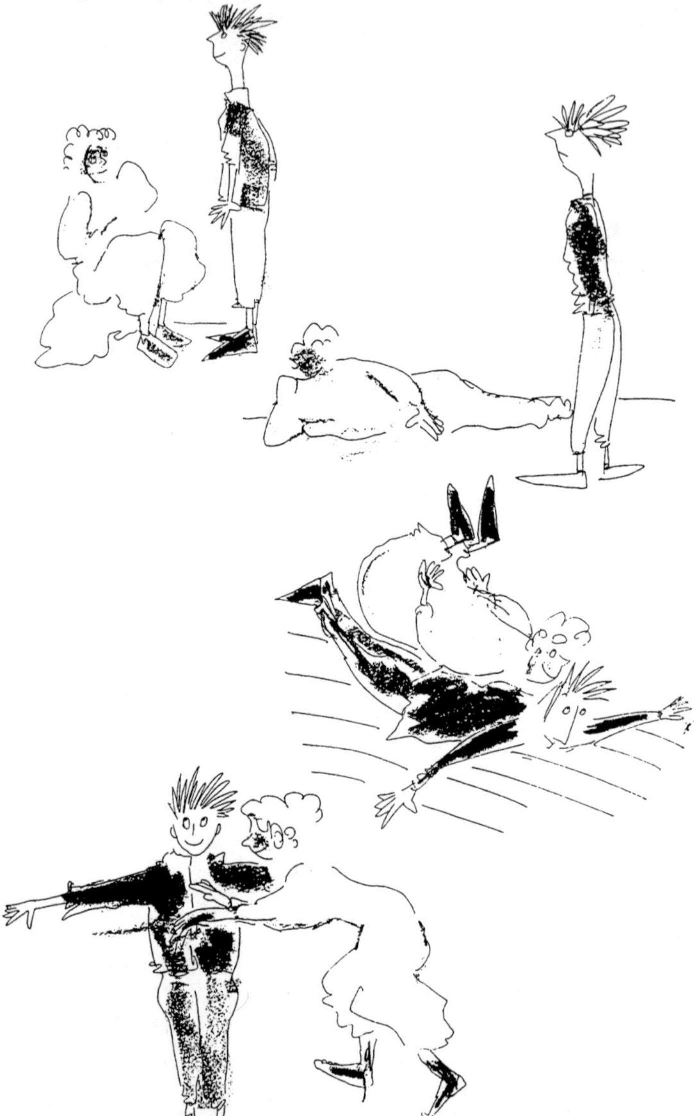

For Sharon

If I were a tree and you were the wind
And my roots did deep into earth descend
You could pass through my branches whenever you pleased
Caress me and help shed my autumn leaves
We could dance in the night sky under the stars
Nothing could stop such exquisite lovers
My branches would grow and rest and bend
If I were a tree and you were the wind

If you were a boat and I were the sea
You could travel the world on top of me
I could rock you and sway you and lead you to cover
Take you to magical lands undiscovered
You'd learn of the storms, the waves and the tides
Travelling near, or travelling wide
You could sail and moor as long as you pleased
If you were a boat, and I were the sea

If you were the coals and I were the flame
We'd be safe from winter's snow and rain
We'd have our guests come warm their souls
Wandering down their winding roads
We'd light up any endless night
Melt down any walls of ice
The fire would shimmer both our names
If you were the coals, and I were the flame

If you were the earth and I were a seed
I'd find a fertile place for me
I'd be a crop of corn or hay
And draw your nourishment every day
After harvest I'd return
To nourish you, the earth – we'd learn
To grow and change and let things be
If you were the earth and I were a seed

If you were here or I were there
And poets lived without a care
If cats and birds had morning tea
And nuns would live in revelry
You'd be the wind and I the tree
You a boat and I the sea
I'd be the flame on your coals, and
The seed inside your deep, rich land
Now we can but work and strive
To keep our own flames burning live
To seek out trees and lands and seas
And know we'll meet in some of these

My Muse

My Muse sits in a smoky den
With a hookah pipe and a greedy yen
For all sensation, good or bad,
Not caring that it's driven her mad.

My Muse sits on a rock by the ocean
Calmly while the storm's commotion
Drenches her till she's nearly drowned,
Yet smiling she is, as she steps down.

My Muse walks with bloody feet
A thousand miles to her retreat
Where she can sleep a thousand years
And in her dreams, confront her fears.

My Muse laughs a roar of thunder
With foulest breath she tears asunder
All illusion sitting tight
Which dares to try to hide the night.

My Muse cries her tears of acid
Searing through existence placid
She leaves the scars but helps to heal
The driving, vital desire to feel.

My Muse is sagging, ancient, wrinkled
Her wisdom tears away my blinkers
Though she may seem a cursed blight
Into Truth she grants me insight.

My Muse will not let me slide
Into comfort, she derides
Complacency, self-satisfaction
And pushes, pushes for reaction.

I thank my Muse for all of this
Although at times her unsolicited kiss
Sends me reeling or knocks me out
It helps me bypass my self-doubt.

The Dreamer

The dreamer laughed, the dreamer sighed,
She threw her head behind and cried
And thus she danced and danced around
Her head a-grinning on the ground

Smiling long from ear to ear
At this relief from body fear,
'Oh tell me when it's time for tea
And I will join you readily.'

The clock upon the silent wall
Ticked by the hours, yet no call
To this lone head upon the floor
Like a long lost meteor

The dancer danced out through the door
No means to ask a mere 'wherefore?'
Vibrant as a new found joy
Light as a bobbing floating buoy

Gliding down the stairs like treacle
Whirring like a lost canticle
Through the corridors all shaking
At this monstrous undertaking

The head by now had gone to sleep
With no body to upkeep
What blissful dreams of love and power
Of lands that yield every flower!

The dancer neared the street side door
No thought or worry anymore
In the street the form went sailing
Jumping, leaping, never failing

People outside ran full screaming
Wondering if their eyes deceiving
Played them tricks of wizardry
With such a sight of revelry

Dancing in, around the houses
Weaving through the laundered blouses
On the washing lines so neat
Now whisked and scattered in the street

The Lord Mayor spluttered from a stage
'This must desist, this vile outrage
To human thought and etiquette.
It's just not done without a head!'

The form went whirling, quite uncaring
Not anybody's eyes worth sparing
Through the fossilising bureaux
Upsetting all the river bateaux

Kicking mud at pinstriped suits
Knocking down the new recruits,
Slamming windows, tweaking hair,
Spreading chaos everywhere.

And all through this the head lay sleeping
Snoring sweetly in such keeping,
Mindless to these acts and deeds.
Oblivion! A simple need

The Lord Mayor with his tie askew
Told the crowd what they should do
Find the head and grab the body
Bring them for his custody.

Too late for either these to be,
The head had rolled on wilfully
The body was too swift to nab
And sought settings far less drab.

The village scoured town and land,
Dug a beach's worth of sand
Felled a forest full of trees,
But head nor body did they see.

There was no dreamer anymore
The head just rolls forever more
The body muses never more
And dances, dances, ever more.

Wear R U

I looked behind the curtains and I searched behind the
chairs,
I even pulled the ceiling down and took apart the stairs.
I undid all the cushions and was starting to despair
No matter what I scrutinised, you simply were not there.

I raised the rugs, removed the rags and ransacked every
room,
Interrogating as I went the roses in full bloom.
Had they seen you walking by or flying on a broom?
Their silence only lent to my increasing sense of doom.

This was by now too much for me, my mind was growing
turbid.
I dug the garden, stopping when I saw this to be morbid.
Surely all my labours could not finish unrewarded?
Perhaps my pleas should be succinct,
Perhaps more deftly worded?

Should I seek you spouting words of promises and money?
Would I reach you if my questions swam in sticky honey?
You're not the kind who likes to see a lover beg on knees
And normally do not receive a nervous wreck with glee.

Was all this work at finding you successful? Alas, no
Wherever you had hidden I most surely did not know,
But having torn my house to bits where else was I to go?
And abjectly I sat and shook my head first to, then fro.

Sitting in the chaos I had managed to impart
I yearned intensely to complete this process I did start.
Then quietly I found you, and your presence made me start
Pressing, pulling, settled, as you are, inside my heart.

The Clown On The Merry-Go-Round

I am the clown on the merry-go-round
Whose face goes whizzing by.
I saw you last year and two years before,
But then, it might have been five.

Remember the day all those lifetimes ago
I decided to go for a caper
And purchased a ticket of candyfloss dreams
But was most adamant it was paper.

I kissed you goodbye and faithfully swore
I'd see you in five or ten minutes
And sat on the horse with the endless blue eyes
Whose bridle had emeralds in it.

I waved you each time I rocked by your spot,
You were smiling at first, that I'm sure,
Watching me sail on my wild high belief
With confidence lacking a cure.

Up on to planets of gemstones and gold,
Down into lurex machines
Around and around and around I'd go
And time was like that in a dream.

It took me a while to realise
This merry-go-round would not stop,
It was going too fast to make a jump
And I'd die if I were to fall off.

I'd pass you each time and quickly cry out
'I'll be with you in only a minute!'
How many hours and years hurried by
When you realised I didn't mean it?

Although I was very sincere when I said
The ride would not take very long,
Those endless blue eyes of my fiery ride
Had not mentioned that I could be wrong.

You'd always smile and wave at me,
Stopping to look as I called,
You'd blow me a kiss on a warm summer breeze
In winter, and spring, and the fall.

Then one day as I came around
Your place had no one standing,
'That's odd,' I thought, 'What time is it?
It must be time for landing.'

But the horse it would not stop at all,
Instead increased its speed,
Where had you gone? Were you still there?
A blur was all I could see.

I turned around to see my own
Reflection in those eyes,
Those eyes of endless blue showed me
Quite different for the ride.

My face appeared all white and red,
The mask of a circus clown,
With teardrops sketched in inky blue
And a worried, fretful frown.

My clothes were brightly coloured silks
Just like the gemstone flight,
My shoes were size sixteen or more
And I was three foot high.

And the ride it would not stop, oh no
It would not stop at all
Perhaps one day I'll make the choice
By opting for a fall,

But you won't be there anymore
You'd waited long enough
So if and when I fall I know
No one will pick me up.

Now this clown on the merry-go-round
Whose face goes whizzing by
Does not need ink to mark the tears
She genuinely cries.

The Granite Bird

Maybe if the Granite Bird
Could fly the dying sea
If the broomsticks 'neath my pillow
Could spell from A to Z
If poets served and riders walked
And weasels babysat
I'd sit in thorny trees and say
'What do you think of that?'

When I was younger than nineteen
I set to sail the seas
To find new lands and tales untold
And socks to match my knees.
The boat ride was amazing
As it turned upside down
So was I as I breathed water
And yet I did not drown.

The first land was a paradise
Of mountains and such stuff,
But then I ate some lemons
And said 'I've had enough.'
The next land was much vaster
'Cos it stretched from there to there,
But when a marshmallow beat my head
It was too much to bear.

So on into more foreign lands
Baked lemons and fried soup
Helter skelters, roller coasters
Ferris wheels that loop the loop
And where is this? This alien land
You're no different from the rest,
I'll wait until it's tea time
And then I'll do what's best.

I might butter my hair or climb the stairs
Fifty times plus once for luck
Or stand upon the rooftop
Throwing things and shouting 'DUCK!'
Or walk backwards down the road
So there's no need to say goodbye,
Or do a master thesis
On the ego of a fly,

But what I'd like to do the most
Is make a lot of noise,
Scream and shout and cry and laugh
And break all of my toys.
'Tut, tut,' you'd say, 'Oh, spoilt child,
Behave yourself at once!
Sit in that corner over there
And wear the cap marked "Dunce".'

Oh how boring that would be
So I'll just say 'Oh fudge!'
I'll buy a silver big wig
And call myself a judge.
Then if the Granite Bird
Could fly the dying sea
If the broomsticks 'neath my pillow
Could spell from A to Z
If poets served and riders walked
And weasels babysat
I'd sit in thorny trees and say
'What do you think of that?'